HEROIN

Susan Elliot-Wright

WITHDRAWN

W

HODDER
Wayland

an imprint of Hodder Children's Books

White-Thomson Publishing Ltd,
2-3 St Andrew's Place, Lewes,
East Sussex BN7 1UP

Published in Great Britain in 2004 by Hodder
Wayland, an imprint of Hodder Children's
Books.

This book was produced for White-Thomson
Publishing Ltd by Ruth Nason.

Design: Carole Binding
Picture research: Glass Onion Pictures

British Library Cataloguing in Publication Data
Susan Elliot-Wright
    Heroin. - (Health Issues)
    1. Heroin habit - Juvenile literature
    2. Heroin - Physiological effect -
    Juvenile literature I. Title
    613.8'3

ISBN 0 7502 4487 9

Printed by C & C Offset Printing, China

Hodder Children's Books
A division of Hodder Headline Limited
338 Euston Road, London NW1 3BH

Acknowledgements

The author and publishers thank the following for their permission to reproduce photographs and
illustrations: Camera Press: page 19; Corbis Images: pages 43 (Lawrence Manning), 50 (Chuck
Savage); Photofusion: pages 3 and 30 (Colin Edwards), 52 (Ulrike Preuss); Popperfoto.com: pages 5,
15, 21, 23, 49b, 54; Rex Features: cover and pages 1, 17, 24, 27, 36, 47, 48; Science Photo Library:
pages 13 (Michael Donne), 34 (St Mary's Hospital Medical School), 37 (Penny Tweedie), 41 (Faye
Norman); Topham: page 7 (Science Museum London/HIP); Topham/Chapman: page 39;
Topham/ImageWorks: pages 4, 33, 44-5, 57, 59; Topham/PA: page 49t; Topham Picturepoint: pages
8, 11, 28. The illustrations on pages 25 and 29 are by Carole Binding.

Note: Photographs illustrating the case studies in this book were posed by models.

Every effort has been made to trace copyright holders. However, the publishers apologise for any
unintentional omissions and would be pleased in such cases to add an acknowledgement in any
future editions.

Contents

Introduction
What is heroin?

You've probably heard quite a lot about heroin, and may already know that it is an extremely dangerous drug. It is illegal to use heroin recreationally – that is, in order to experience a 'high'– rather than as medication, prescribed by a doctor. Heroin has been classified as 'class A' in Britain and 'schedule 1' in the USA. These classifications are given to the group of drugs that are considered to be the most dangerous. Anyone caught in possession of, or selling, one of these drugs, faces serious penalties – up to life in prison for selling the drug to someone else.

Heroin is made from the juice of the opium poppy, refined into a powder, which is then smoked, or heated and inhaled, or dissolved and injected. It is highly addictive, can kill at first use and often wrecks the lives of those who become dependent on it. Heroin has been around for about 100 years, and its use has grown since the 1970s, leading to serious drug problems in many parts of the world.

Raw opium
Cuts are made in the seedpod of an opium poppy, and its juice oozes out. The juice is collected and can be processed into heroin powder.

Heroin use among celebrities, particularly those from the music world, has frequently hit the headlines. There have been stories of ruined lives and careers and heroin-linked deaths such as that of the Nirvana singer, Kurt Cobain. But most heroin users are ordinary people who start off thinking they will 'just try it once'. There are currently an estimated 250,000 heroin users in the UK and around 800,000 in the USA.

An average dependent user spends around £10,000 a year on their habit, and three-quarters of this money, according to recent government research, comes from crime. Many users end up in prison, homeless, jobless, in poor health and with no contact with their families. Around a third will die as a result of heroin use. Chapter 4 looks at what heroin can do to someone's body, and Chapter 5 looks more at what happens to the life of the user.

Why, you might wonder, if heroin is so terrible, does anybody use it at all? When heroin is first used, it gives the user a powerful, sudden feeling of pleasure and wellbeing, described as a 'high' or 'rush'. Chapter 3 explains the effect heroin has on the brain to cause this and to make the person associate heroin with extreme pleasure. It is often people who live in unhappy or under-privileged circumstances who are most attracted to drugs, seeing them as a way of escaping the pain of their lives. The sad fact is that the pleasure heroin gives evaporates quickly, and the pain returns, with the addition of unpleasant withdrawal symptoms which only disappear (temporarily) with more heroin. This is how addiction begins.

Addicted

Many heroin users inject the drug. It is highly addictive and addiction develops quickly. Obtaining and taking heroin become the focus of the person's life.

In recent years, much of the discussion in schools about drugs has focused on cannabis and so-called 'clubbing' drugs such as ecstasy. Some experts fear that this has resulted in today's young people not being aware of the dangers of heroin. Chapter 6 addresses the issue of education and information, and asks whether better drugs education would help reduce the number of people becoming addicted.

'We talk about drugs at school, but I don't know that much about heroin. I read about it in the papers sometimes, and it sounds scary.'
(Charlie, aged 15)

Depending on where you live, you may be aware of drug treatment or rehabilitation centres in your area. You may even know someone who is dependent on heroin, or who has tried it. It is often the case that, when somebody has a problem with drugs or alcohol, they are unable to see that problem clearly for themselves. This may mean that what they say about a certain drug, or a particular aspect of drug use, is less than accurate. The purpose of this book is to provide straightforward information about heroin and its effects on the individual and on society. Hopefully, it will answer any questions you may have and clear up some of the myths about heroin use – like, for example, 'you can't get hooked unless you inject'; (you can).

The book will also show that, even when people have reached rock-bottom as a result of addiction, it is possible to recover and lead a worthwhile life. The accounts given by addicts, ex-addicts and the families of addicts will show both the horror and the hope.

Help

If you need more information about heroin, or if you know someone who might need help, the organizations listed on page 62 may be useful.

1 Heroin's forerunners A brief history of opiates

Heroin is one of a group of drugs called opiates. The name 'opiate' comes from the opium poppy, which grows across central and southeast Asia. The seedpod of the poppy produces a sticky substance called opium, which has been widely used both recreationally and as a medicine for centuries. Opiates, including heroin, morphine and codeine, are derived from opium. There are also synthetic (man-made) opiates, such as pethidine and methadone.

The use of opium in ancient civilizations

The first records of the use of opium as a painkiller, or analgesic, date back 6,000 years to the Sumerians. They referred to the opium poppy as 'the joy plant'. Ancient Egyptian and Babylonian writings also contain references to opium preparations for the relief of pain, and to an accompanying sense of wellbeing and calm. These ancient peoples either ate parts of the flower or made them into a drink.

Opium use in China

In around the seventh or eighth century AD, Arab traders introduced opium to China, where it continued to be used as a medicine, but where recreational use began to grow steadily. Around this time it was discovered that igniting and smoking the opium produced a more powerful effect, and the habit of opium smoking spread. Opium pipes became a sort of fashion accessory, ranging from plain clay or bamboo pipes to elaborately decorated and bejewelled creations called 'hookahs'. The type of pipe would reflect the wealth of the user.

Opium pipe
This Chinese pipe for smoking opium was made from ivory, with an ornate metal mount.

Opium makes users sleepy, lethargic and uninterested in the world around them. It reduces the inclination and ability to work, study, maintain relationships or have sex. The desire to eat may disappear, and even if it doesn't, the body's ability to digest food is weakened. Long-term use of opium impairs many of the body's physical and psychological functions. Opium is also highly addictive, which means that once someone starts to use it regularly, they may find it extremely difficult to stop. At first, this is because the drug gives them a good feeling, but eventually they take it because if they don't, they start to suffer unpleasant 'withdrawal symptoms'.

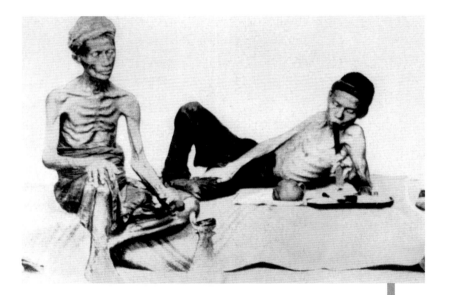

Western doctors working in China at the end of the nineteenth century reported that opium was 'a ruinous drug'. One is quoted as saying, 'It destroys morals, makes physical wrecks and severs social relationships.' Around this time in China, an estimated 70,000 or 80,000 opium addicts were dying yearly. The effect on Chinese society was devastating. In order to finance their addiction, male opium users would sell everything – sometimes even their wives and children. When everything was gone, they would turn to begging and stealing. Women addicts often turned to prostitution.

Physical wrecks
This photograph of opium smokers in China shows how opium took over the lives of users, often at the expense of their health.

The Chinese Opium Wars

Until the eighteenth century, trade between Britain and China was mostly in China's favour. The Chinese sold tea, which had become fashionable in Europe, and beautiful silk and porcelain, but they had little interest in buying what they regarded as inferior British products. Then the British began to export opium from India, at that time a British colony, to China. Opium became popular as a recreational drug, and addiction began to ravage parts of China, especially around Canton (now known as Guangzhou), where most overseas trade took place. Britain's opium exports to China resulted in two wars.

The First Opium War, 1839-42

In 1839, Lin Ze-xu was appointed to stamp out the opium trade. He wrote to Queen Victoria, asking her to stop Britain's merchants from trafficking 'this poisonous drug'. The Queen ignored him. He then demanded that the traders hand over their opium stocks, but they held off for six weeks before finally giving up more than 20,000 barrels of opium which was then destroyed. Lin Ze-xu refused to allow the traders to buy tea, rice or silk for export until they signed a pledge promising not to bring any more opium into the country. This sparked an aggressive response from British opium traders and the British military, who landed on and occupied Hong Kong. The antiquated Chinese army and navy were no match for the British military, and China was defeated. The war ended in 1842 with the Treaty of Nanking, which not only gave the British trading rights in five ports, but also gave control of Hong Kong to 'her Britannic Majesty, her heirs and successors'. (Control of Hong Kong was returned to the Chinese in 1997.)

The Second Opium War, 1856-60

In 1856 the British wanted to extend trading rights and attacked China again. The Chinese were defeated and forced to sign the treaties of Tiensin (1858), which opened up more ports to Western trade and residence, and provided freedom of movement for Christian missionaries. Further negotiations led to the importation of opium being legalized. At first the Chinese refused to comply, but after Peking was captured and the emperor's summer palace burned down, they signed the Peking Convention (1860) agreeing to observe the treaties of Tiensin.

Opium use in the West

In the West, opium use became a widespread problem in the nineteenth century. 'Opium dens', where people could go to smoke opium, became popular in Europe and the USA, especially in areas with an established Chinese community. But one of the main problems was the use of opium in medicines. Opium-related preparations were used for a variety of ailments, including tuberculosis, malaria and diarrhoea. Many 'over-the-counter' medicines contained opium or morphine. With names like 'Mrs Winslow's Soothing Syrup', 'Ayer's Cherry Pectoral' and 'Atkinson's Royal Infant Preservative', they sounded harmless enough, and were advertised as 'cough mixtures', 'painkillers' and 'women's friends'. People at the time did not realize that something that could 'cure' could actually be harmful.

Laudanum – a Victorian cure-all

Laudanum was a mixture of opium, alcohol and spices. It was originally thought of as a 'working-class' drug because it was very cheap, but it soon became popular right across Victorian society. Like the various medicines

Babies and children on drugs

Nannies, nursemaids and exhausted mothers calmed restless and crying babies by giving them spoonfuls of laudanum to help them sleep. Sales of 'Godfrey's Cordial', an opium-based colic remedy, were high. One druggist in the North of England admitted to selling half a gallon each week. Another sold 400 gallons of laudanum annually.

'Poppy tea' was also given to children in some parts of England and doctors noted how infants in those areas seemed 'shrank up into little old men' or 'wizened like monkeys'. Many babies died as a result of overdose, and more still died of starvation. A doctor investigating the high infant mortality rate noted how children 'kept in a state of continuous narcotism will be thereby disinclined for food'. Death from malnutrition was likely to result.

containing opium, both laudanum and raw opium were easy to buy, at pharmacies and in grocery stores. Some doctors prescribed laudanum for headaches, sleeplessness or depression, often dispensing the drug themselves. Many upper-class Victorian ladies became increasingly dependent on laudanum to relieve the stress and boredom of their daily lives.

Sharpening the senses

Laudanum was also widely used in artistic circles, particularly by writers and poets who felt that it sharpened the senses and made them more creative. Charles Dickens, Samuel Taylor Coleridge and Lord Byron were known to be users. Lewis Carroll was said to go to opium dens, and may well have written *Alice in Wonderland* under the influence of laudanum. The dream-like world in which Alice exists certainly suggests a drug-induced state, and the book may even refer to smoking opium:

'She peeped over the edge of the mushroom, and her eyes immediately met those of a large blue caterpillar that was sitting on the top, with its arms folded, quietly smoking a long hookah, and taking not the smallest notice of anything else.'

The blue caterpillar
The sleepy, laid-back state of this character in 'Alice in Wonderland' sounds similar to the state of someone smoking opium.

Thomas De Quincey (1785-1859), the author of *Confessions of an English Opium Eater* (1821), gives some clue as to why the drug was so popular:

'...the opium eater...feels that the diviner part of his nature is paramount; that is, the moral affections are in a state of cloudless serenity; and over all is the light of the majestic intellect...'

But people soon became addicted to the drug, partly because the body quickly developed a tolerance to it. This means it required more each time to get the same effect. Writer Wilkie Collins (1824-89) used laudanum to kill the intense pain he suffered as a result of rheumatic gout. He carried around a silver flask of laudanum from which he needed to drink ever-increasing amounts in order to gain relief. By the end of his life, according to his surgeon Sir William Fergusson, he was consuming enough each day to kill twelve people. Although this may well have been an exaggeration, it is probably accurate to say that, over the years, his body had built up such a tolerance that it was able to stand amounts that would certainly have killed someone who was not used to those quantities. People who die from opiate abuse usually die of organ failure, often failure of the heart or lungs.

Morphine

Today, the use of raw opium has virtually disappeared in the West. Drug manufacturers convert most opium into the legal painkiller codeine, although large quantities of morphine, a more powerful analgesic, are also produced.

Morphine was first separated from opium by a German pharmacist in 1805. He named it Morphium, after Morpheus, the Greek god of dreams. Morphine is used legally to treat severe pain such as that experienced after an operation, but a side effect of its painkilling action is a feeling of detachment and euphoria and the drug is highly addictive. Morphine is not usually imported illegally, but addicts do frequently steal it from hospital pharmacies.

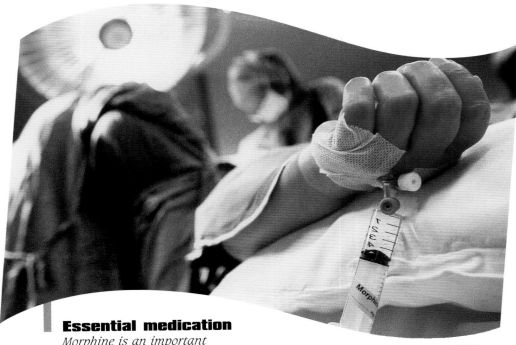

Essential medication

*Morphine is an important
painkilling drug, used
in hospitals.*

Ironically, before its addictive
nature became known, morphine was
often given to treat opium addiction
and alcoholism. The idea was that
the morphine would relieve
the withdrawal symptoms
experienced when the person
stopped taking the substance to
which they were addicted. Then,
once their body had become used
to not receiving the addictive
substance, the morphine treatment
could be stopped. Even when it
was realized that morphine itself
was addictive, the treatment was
still used in some cases because
morphine was thought to be less harmful
to the body than opium.

Fact file

*In China at the start of the
twentieth century, Western
missionaries handed out
morphine pills as remedies
for opium addiction. In
fact, the pills were used
recreationally as a
substitute for opium and
soon became known as
'Jesus-Opium'.*

Synthetic opiates

These are man-made painkiller drugs whose action is similar to that of opium-derived drugs. For example, pethidine, like morphine or heroin, produces a 'rush' – a sense of instant euphoria – immediately after it is taken, usually by injection. Because this feeling of wellbeing is so desirable, recreational users are keen to repeat the experience, which often leads to addiction. Pethidine is still widely used for pain relief for women in labour; it works by altering the woman's perception of the pain, thus increasing her ability to bear it.

Methadone is another synthetic opiate. It can also produce a rush when injected, but it is not as strong. Its painkilling effects can last for up to 12 hours.

Tolerance to synthetic opiates develops quickly as the power of the rush or 'hit' quickly diminishes. But tolerance is lost again fairly quickly, so there is a strong risk of overdose.

When the hypodermic syringe was developed in the mid-nineteenth century, people began to inject pure morphine. It was mistakenly thought that injecting was not as addictive as swallowing morphine pills. Use of the drug as a legal medicine to treat wounded servicemen during the American Civil War (1861-65) led to extremely high levels of addiction, which became known as 'the soldiers' disease'. A hundred years later, soldiers fighting in the Vietnam War also became addicted.

Heroin: a cure for morphine addiction

Heroin was originally developed towards the end of the nineteenth century, as a treatment for addiction to morphine. It is made by adding chemicals to morphine, to make it more easily absorbed by the body. Heroin was thought to be a safe and non-addictive alternative, whereas, in fact, it is at least as addictive as morphine, and has become known as one of the most dangerous and destructive drugs available today.

2 Heroin use today
Supply and demand

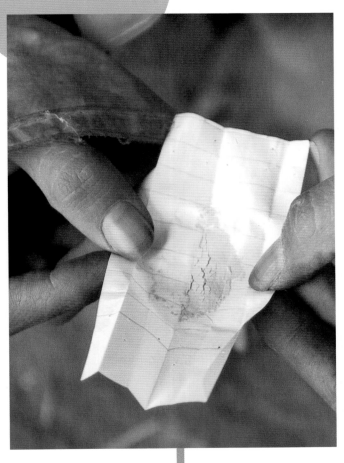

By the time heroin – also known as Smack, Brown, H, Skag, Horse, Junk, Jack – reaches our streets, it is in the form of a white or brownish powder, usually sold in a 'bag' or 'wrap' containing a single dose or 'hit'. Pure heroin is white, but this is rarely sold on the street. Most street heroin varies from off-white to dark brown, because of impurities left from the manufacturing process or because of the presence of additives.

Street heroin is often mixed or 'cut' with other substances – anything from sugar or powdered milk to scouring powder, brick dust, glass or rat poison. Traditionally, the purity of heroin in a wrap ranged from one to 10 per cent. More recently, as the cost of buying heroin in bulk has fallen, dealers have been able to make their profit without using large quantities of additives. This means that the purity of heroin in a wrap may now be as high as 98 per cent.

It is impossible for users to know exactly what they are buying, or the strength of the heroin they are getting. If they think they have established a 'safe' dose, and then one day they take heroin that is much purer than they are used to, the result will be overdose and, possibly, death.

A heroin wrap
Heroin users normally buy the drug in single doses. The amount of the powder that is actually heroin varies.

Heroin slang: words you might hear on the street

Junkie – *heroin addict*
Shooting up – *injecting heroin*
Chasing the dragon – *heating heroin and inhaling the vapours produced*
To cut heroin – *to mix or 'bulk' it with another substance, in order to increase profit*
Cooking up – *preparing heroin for injection*
Works – *name for the paraphernalia associated with injecting*
Cold turkey – *name for withdrawal symptoms (which often include chills and 'gooseflesh')*
Clean – *having come off heroin*

There are several ways of taking heroin. The powder can be snorted, smoked, heated on foil and inhaled (known as 'chasing the dragon'), or mixed with water, heated and then injected. Another form, 'black tar heroin', which is manufactured mainly in Mexico, has become increasingly available, particularly in the USA. It looks just like it sounds – black and sticky, like roofing tar. It is usually dissolved, diluted and injected.

What's the attraction?

Heroin is a fast-acting drug which affects the brain's pleasure centre (more about this in Chapter 4), producing a 'rush' – a surge of pleasure that may be accompanied by a warm, contented feeling, a detachment from the 'real world' and relief from anxiety. The effects depend on how the drug is taken. Injection produces the most intense response most quickly – usually within a few seconds.

On the down side, users, especially those using the drug for the first time, may experience nausea and vomiting. Speech may be slurred, the eyelids may droop and the user may suffer chronic constipation. Repeated use has devastating consequences, both to health and to everyday life. The drug is viciously addictive, and addiction develops quickly. As the need for the drug becomes the most important thing in their life, many users turn to crime in order to finance their habit. Heroin addicts often end up with no job or home, and may be reduced to begging on the streets. Around two per cent of users who inject the drug die each year.

How does heroin end up on our streets?

Much of the world's heroin – 75 per cent – comes from Afghanistan, which is the source of 90 per cent of Britain's supply. The other main sources are Pakistan, Mexico and, more recently, Colombia, which is the main source of heroin entering the USA. The length of the 'heroin chain' – the chain of people involved in bringing heroin to our streets – can vary. It may have as few as five links: opium farmer-manufacturer-importer-dealer-user.

Heroin production begins with the farming of opium poppies. The farmer collects raw opium by making cuts in the pod of the poppy. Over the next few days, the sticky opium oozes out of the cuts, and each morning, the farmer scrapes this off. Farmers usually then sell their raw opium at local markets to opium traders, or they may carry out the next stage themselves.

Fact file

Until 2000, it was legal for farmers in Afghanistan to grow and sell their opium. In 2000, cultivation (growing) of opium poppies became illegal, but trading in opium was still permitted. In 2002, trading in opium was also banned, although it still continues on a large scale.

Opium for sale
This farmer is displaying the raw opium he has for sale at a local market in Afghanistan.

This next stage is processing. It is carried out by the farmers or local traders in makeshift laboratories, using basic techniques and equipment. The raw opium is converted into morphine base by dissolving it in boiling water, adding lime (a white substance used in making cement and sometimes as a fertilizer), filtering, then adding concentrated ammonia before heating again. The morphine solidifies and settles at the bottom of the pot. It is then wrapped into blocks and dried in the sun before being sold on to manufacturers with slightly more sophisticated laboratories, where it is further refined. The base is heated and simple chemicals such as acetic acid are added. Finally, sodium carbonate, a common ingredient in soaps, is added to form heroin base.

'Smoking heroin' is made by mixing heroin base with hydrochloric acid and addictive substances such as caffeine. The resulting paste dries into brownish lumps that are crushed ready for sale. This heroin, sometimes known as 'brown sugar' due to its appearance, is around 20-30 per cent pure.

The white powder that is suitable for injection is made by adding hydrochloric acid and ether to the heroin base. It is then filtered, dried and compressed into bricks. This heroin has a purity of 80-90 per cent.

'It's all down to greed. All along the chain, the price goes up, with everyone making a fat profit – except for the poor devils who grow the stuff and the kids who die on the street after taking it.'
(Andy Willis, 'Drug Squad' detective)

Manufacturers in Afghanistan may sell their heroin for £600 per kilo to brokers, who ship it for around £7,000 per kilo to importers in destination countries. These brokers often recruit couriers, sometimes called 'mules', to carry heroin in small amounts. Large quantities enter the destination countries by various routes, smuggled in amongst legitimate imported goods or hidden in luggage, in boats, cars and lorries. Mid-level distributors now purchase the drug for about £22,000 a kilo. At this point, it may be bulked out with cutting agents and sold to street-level dealers for around £1,000 an ounce – that's £35,000 a kilo, a mark-up of roughly 60 times the original price!

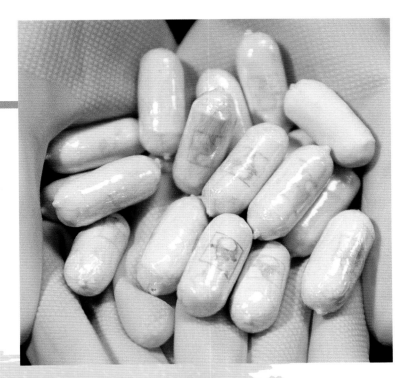

Heroin haul

Customs officers seized these portions of heroin wrapped in latex. They would have been swallowed by people recruited by drug smugglers to carry them from one country to another.

Drug smugglers

Drug smugglers are constantly looking for new ways of getting heroin through customs. Couriers or 'mules' can carry quite large quantities either in suitcases or in their stomachs – in latex balloons or condoms which they swallow before boarding a plane. On arrival, they retrieve the heroin by making themselves vomit or by taking laxatives and passing it out via the bowel.

In many cases, the smuggled heroin is discovered when the courier becomes ill due to heroin leaking into the stomach. Often couriers have been rushed to hospital with stomach pains, only to be arrested after an X-ray or surgery reveals the hidden drug. Many couriers have died after the package has burst, flooding their system with heroin and causing a fatal overdose.

In March 2003, a man was arrested for trying to smuggle 18kg of highly refined heroin – worth more than $6 million – into India. It was hidden in almond shells.

Heroin is bought on the street by the user, who may buy more than he or she needs in order to sell some on for a small profit, to help fund their own habit. The cost of a single dose of heroin has fallen considerably due to the increased availability. Heroin can now be found for as little as £10 a wrap.

It has often been suggested that a dealer will 'push' heroin – that is, give away a 'free sample'. The idea is that the person will enjoy the free hit so much that they will be keen to try again and will buy the next dose, quickly becoming addicted and providing the dealer with a new customer. Some drug organizations suggest this is a myth, claiming that one hit does not guarantee addiction and that 'free trials' are only given between dealers and users who have built up a relationship over some time.

When is heroin not heroin?

In 2002, a British journalist went out on the streets in various cities to see what drugs were available and what they cost. When the heroin he purchased was analysed, it was found that the amount and purity varied enormously from place to place. One 'half-gram' bag of heroin actually contained 0.04g – less than one-twentieth of a gram. Some 'heroin' was in fact mainly pulverized stone and glass.

'I started dealing'

'I was on H for years, and I was always obsessed with how I was going to afford the next hit. I sold everything I owned, and a lot of what other people owned, too. I even nicked stuff from my Nan. Eventually, I started dealing. Only small amounts – I couldn't afford to buy a lot in one go. But it was a good way to increase my income.

I knew some of the stuff I bought was cut with rubbish – sometimes it was glucose or flour, other times it could be talcum powder, dustbin freshener, brick dust. People sometimes ask me if I ever worry about what that junk might have done to the guys who used it, and yeah, I do worry about it now. But at the time, all you care about is the next hit. The kid could fall down and die in front of you, and you wouldn't care – as long as he'd paid you up front, of course. It was a bad time.'
(Tony, aged 23, ex-heroin user)

A lethal crop

You might wonder why farmers continue to grow opium that they know will be made into heroin. The reason is that they can earn far more by growing opium than by growing other crops, although their earnings are still fairly low.

In July 2000, the growing of opium poppies was banned in Afghanistan, under the Taliban government. As a result, the production of opium fell to 185 tonnes in 2001. However, because of the smaller quantities available, the price of heroin shot up. Opium farmers received little compensation for their lost livelihood, and many were close to ruin. With no incentive to observe the ban, many replanted their fields to take advantage of the higher prices. The result was a bumper crop – around 3,500 tonnes – in 2002, leading to a fall in prices and a flood of high-quality heroin on the streets.

'I picked coffee beans for a living, but the price kept falling and in the end there was no work. I have a wife and five children to feed. With poppies, I can make a living. I can even save a little.'
(Tehru Akran, Afghan opium farmer)

Destroying heroin

In July 2002, as a sign of their determination to crack down on the drug trade, the authorities in Afghanistan lit a bonfire of refined opium that had been seized from local traders.

3 Why do people use heroin?
The slippery slope of addiction

Young people try drugs for a number of reasons, but the most common is curiosity – 'What will happen if I take this?' 'How will it make me feel?' In a British survey on this subject in spring 2002, 75 per cent of those taking part cited curiosity as the main reason they had tried illegal drugs, with 22 per cent blaming peer pressure and 3 per cent a 'desire to emulate heroes'. The vast majority of people who try a drug do not become long-term users.

Many drugs produce a sense of euphoria – an intense feeling of pleasure and general wellbeing, sometimes described as being 'high'. Some drugs make users feel more relaxed, others make users feel lively, confident and full of energy. But what all addictive drugs have in common is that the feeling of pleasure is soon followed by the opposite feeling. The user begins to 'come down', often experiencing extreme tiredness, depression or deeply unpleasant physical symptoms. With heroin, the 'high' is sudden, sometimes described as a 'rush' of pleasure. Users talk of a feeling of escape, of complete, worry-free detachment. But coming down can be devastating; the high is followed by a 'crash'.

'I know these guys who smoke heroin and I must admit, I'm tempted just to find out what it feels like. I think I'd be too scared to try it, though.' (Fin, aged 15)

Heroin culture

The story of Becky, on page 23, is typical of many heroin users: an unhappy home life, running away to a big city and finding themselves lonely and vulnerable. Young people who end up sleeping on the streets often find themselves part of a group that may include people who abuse heroin and other drugs. Heroin offers an immediate sense of wellbeing and escape from real life, including problems. For this reason, it is often people who are already on the edge of society who are attracted to the drug – for example, offenders, those without jobs or homes, or those suffering from depression or other mental health problems. As a result, heroin users, linked by a feeling of being outside of society, soon form friendships among themselves.

The shared obsession with finding the next fix means they are all 'in the same boat', and this leads to a sense of bonding and belonging.

Friendship?
A shared need for heroin brings people together.

'Something special'

'I used to live in a house, once, with my parents. It was only three years ago, but it seems much longer. I ran away from home after a fight with my mum's boyfriend. They asked me to go back, but they didn't really want me. I've never got on with my parents, but things just got worse. Anyway, I wanted to prove I didn't need them.

I'd smoked a bit of weed before, but then I met a guy who said that weed was for kids, and that if I wanted something really special, he could arrange it. So I tried heroin. You're told it's a killer – the worst thing you can do. So it attracts you all the more. I only wanted to try it once, partly to see what it was like, partly just to do something dangerous. Also, I thought it would be cool. Now look at me. I used to think I'd get married one day, perhaps have kids, but no-one would come near me now. I've got friends on the street – well, they're not friends, really. We shoot up together, but if I died, they wouldn't really care – probably wouldn't even notice. I might get AIDS. Might already have it, for all I know. I don't think about the future any more. My last fix was five hours ago, so I'll need more soon. That's my future.'
(Becky, aged 19)

Other users become a substitute for family and friends, and daily life becomes a constant challenge to find money for heroin. Days may consist of begging, stealing or prostitution in order to fund the habit. With no worthwhile occupation and so little social contact, users may find comfort in the rituals of buying heroin and preparing it for injection. Addicts may become almost as dependent on the rituals as on the drug itself.

Petty thieving

Often the motive for stealing is that the object taken can be sold, providing money to buy heroin or other drugs.

One thing leads to another

Some drugs – cannabis, for example – are often seen by young people as 'soft' drugs, which won't do them any harm. Indeed, there are many people who believe that using such drugs should not be a criminal offence. However, many who have come into contact with the horror of heroin addiction, or have experienced it themselves, argue that so-called soft drugs can put users on the path to more dangerous drugs as they seek increasingly stronger mind-altering effects. It could be that using cannabis involves people in buying illegal drugs, making it more likely that they will be offered heroin at some point. Drug organizations agree that almost all heroin users started on cannabis. However, only a small proportion of those who use cannabis go on to use heroin.

How addiction works

Addiction is defined by the medical profession as 'the repeated compulsive use of a substance despite unpleasant or even life-threatening consequences'. Experts still don't know as much as they would like about the nature of addiction – there is little research on the subject – but they are agreed that it usually involves both physical and psychological dependence.

Psychological dependence

Heroin mimics the action of endorphins, which are chemicals that occur naturally in the brain. Endorphins are the body's natural 'feel good' chemicals. They block pain and induce feelings of pleasure and wellbeing. The brain produces these chemicals in larger quantities when we do something enjoyable, such as play our favourite sports, go dancing or laugh – the natural 'highs' of daily life. When these highs occur, or when pain is relieved, the endorphins stimulate the production of another chemical called dopamine, which creates vivid, positive memories of the experience.

Dopamine acts as a sort of messenger, telling another part of the brain, 'the reward centre', that you feel great. When someone takes heroin, much more dopamine is released than would occur due to the action of natural endorphins. The user's brain feels intense pleasure during the rush of the heroin hit, and soon begins to associate taking heroin with feeling great. Taking heroin quickly becomes an experience the user is keen to repeat.

Physical dependence

Before long, the body gets used to heroin. This is called tolerance. The brain begins to adapt to the over-

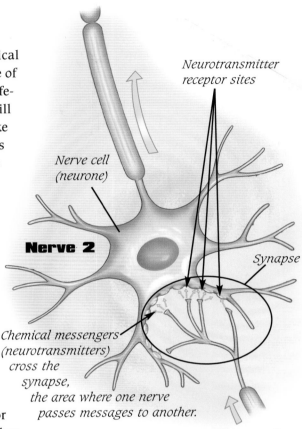

Neurotransmitter receptor sites

Nerve cell (neurone)

Nerve 2

Synapse

Chemical messengers (neurotransmitters) cross the synapse, the area where one nerve passes messages to another.

Nerve 1

Chemical messengers

Nerves in the brain communicate with each other by passing tiny amounts of chemicals between the end of one nerve and the beginning of the next. The result of taking heroin is that a very large amount of the chemical messenger, or neurotransmitter, called dopamine is produced, and this increases the brain's activity.

stimulation of dopamine, and the user needs more and more heroin in order to get the same 'high'. In addition, the user's brain becomes less sensitive to natural endorphins, so unless he or she takes heroin, the brain will not release enough dopamine. As a result, the person is likely to experience feelings of anxiety and despair, and so they take more heroin to relieve those feelings. Very soon, they no longer experience the pleasure that they associate with heroin; they are taking it purely to get rid of the bad feelings – called 'withdrawal symptoms' – that are generated by its use. By this time, they need heroin in order to feel normal. They are now addicted.

Withdrawal symptoms

Withdrawal symptoms can occur within hours of the last use of heroin, although they are usually at their worst between 48 and 72 hours after last use. After this, they begin to ease off over several days. The symptoms include:

- *intense craving for heroin*
- *anxiety*
- *restlessness*
- *insomnia*

- *fever and sweating*
- *aching limbs and painful cramps*
- *vomiting and diarrhoea*
- *chills and shivering.*

Withdrawal is sometimes known as 'cold turkey', due to the chills and goose bumps that appear on the skin.

How fast do people become addicted?

Drug workers suggest that daily heroin use over six to eight weeks is likely to lead to dependence. It varies, depending on a number of factors, including physical make-up, state of mind and social situation. People differ in their sensitivity to all drugs, including alcohol: for instance, some are 'social drinkers' throughout their lives, others become alcoholics or 'alcohol-dependent'. There's no way of knowing in advance how someone may react to any drug, but addicts almost always say that they didn't realize they were becoming addicted until it was too late.

'I never thought it could happen to me'

Matt was studying medicine when he started using heroin. His father was a doctor, and Matt had dreams of becoming a heart surgeon. According to his tutors, he was one of their brightest students. But he was thrown out of medical school in his third year, after becoming addicted to heroin. After living on the streets for a while, he now lives with his family again, but is still fighting his addiction.

'I never thought it could happen to me,' says Matt. 'The first time, I was at a party with a girl in my seminar group. She said that chasing the dragon was safe, and that I'd feel better than I'd ever felt in my life. Well, it didn't feel as great as I thought, and I threw up. But I was intrigued enough to try again, and that time, it was fantastic, incredible. So then I thought, well, I don't spend my money on fancy clothes or anything, so why not? Just at weekends and parties. But after the first few times, it wasn't as good as before, and I was feeing really bad in between, so I started using it more often. At that point, I was still going to lectures. But then even twice a day wasn't helping, and that's when I started injecting. In the end, they threw me out of college. I don't know whether it was because of the heroin or whether it was the stealing – I had to nick stuff because my parents wouldn't give me any more money. I stayed with mates for a while, but most of the time I was sleeping rough. I'm back home now, but I don't know how long I'll stay. It's harder to get a fix down here, and although my parents have been supportive, I know it hurts them to see me like this.'

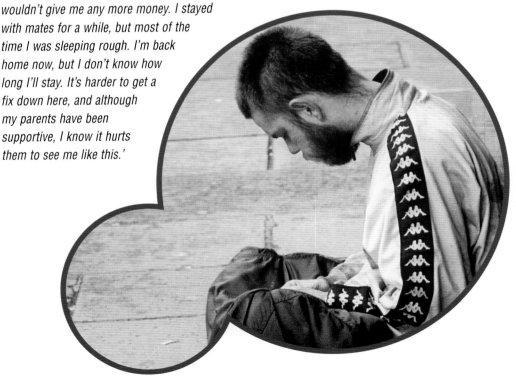

Who uses heroin?

Studies put the average age of first use of heroin at between 18 and 21, although the age at which people first try the drug does seem to be coming down. In a 2001 study in the UK, one per cent of 11-15 year olds claimed to have used heroin in the last year.

Traditionally, heroin use has been associated with deprived areas of towns and cities. However, although studies show that its use is still more prevalent in poorer areas, there is some evidence to suggest that heroin use is increasing in rural areas and across different social groups. One of the reasons for this is possibly the fact that, due to the large crops of opium available in recent years, street heroin is increasing in purity and falling in price. This means that better-quality heroin is available to more people.

Also, the fashion for 'chasing the dragon' – inhaling the vapour from heated heroin – means that it's not necessary to inject the drug. This means that people can use heroin without the health risks associated with injecting, such as HIV and hepatitis. However, many people try inhaling or smoking heroin after assuming, wrongly, that these methods will not lead to addiction. This is quite ironic when you consider that nineteenth-century morphine users actually switched to injecting morphine in the belief that injecting would not lead to addiction.

Chasing the dragon

This means heating heroin and inhaling the fumes. It is no less addictive than injecting the drug.

4 How heroin damages health
A powerful poison

What does heroin do to the user's body?

Heroin enters the user's bloodstream – directly, if it is injected, or via the lungs, if it is smoked or inhaled. It then crosses the 'blood-brain barrier', getting into the brain within 30 seconds. Like all opiates, heroin has a depressant effect on the central nervous system – the system consisting of the brain and spinal cord. This is why opiates work as painkillers: they depress the nerve transmissions that signal pain.

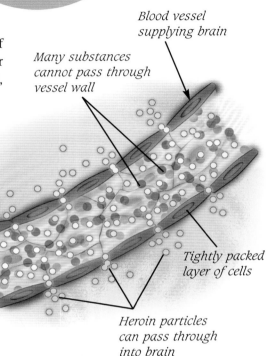

Blood vessel supplying brain

Many substances cannot pass through vessel wall

Tightly packed layer of cells

Heroin particles can pass through into brain

Passing through

The blood vessels that supply the brain are lined with cells which prevent many substances in the blood from crossing into the brain. But this lining is not a barrier for heroin.

Heroin works by attaching to sites called 'opioid receptors', which are part of the body's mechanism for feeling pleasure and relieving pain. These receptors exist because the body produces its own natural chemicals, called endorphins, to kill pain, promote pleasure, control mood and cope with stress. When heroin is taken, the receptors are bombarded, so that the brain's 'pleasure centre' is stimulated to an unnatural degree.

Heroin and the blood-brain barrier

Heroin enters the brain very quickly because it is able to cross what is known as the 'blood-brain barrier'. The tiny blood vessels or capillaries that supply the brain are lined with a tightly packed layer of cells which act as a barrier preventing many substances from crossing into the brain and causing damage. But heroin dissolves in the blood's fatty acids and this enables it to pass through the barrier.

Although heroin stimulates the pleasure centre, it has the opposite (slowing-down) effect on other systems in the body, such as the respiratory, cardio-vascular (controlling the heart and circulation) and digestive systems. It causes a drop in body temperature and slows down breathing so that, after the first euphoric rush, the muscles relax, the limbs feel heavy and the eyelids droop. The user is likely to feel very drowsy – sometimes called being 'on the nod' or 'nodding off', and may feel confused and disorientated. The heart beats much more slowly and weakly and so blood is not circulated properly. In an overdose, breathing may actually stop, and the user dies. Heroin suppresses the digestive system, causing loss of appetite and constipation, which can be severe. Heroin also affects the concentration of hormones in the body, causing irregular periods in women and loss of sexual desire in both sexes.

System slow-down

Heroin slows down all the systems of the body. An overdose can lead to death.

Short-term problems

The first time someone uses heroin, they may vomit or experience severe nausea and dizziness. If they use a needle that has already been used by someone else, there is also the risk of catching infections such as HIV or hepatitis.

Overdose, which may be fatal, is possible at first use, although it is more common in long-term users whose tolerance has decreased as a result of not taking heroin for a while – for example, if they have been in prison, or have been trying to come off the drug. Overdose is also more

Dead in a public toilet

'Adam was a normal lad. He'd just left school and started work in a music store. It wasn't a wonderful job, but he seemed to like it. He made lots of friends, went to lots of parties – I was pleased that he was enjoying himself.

I had no idea he was into drugs until he started stealing from me, taking money out of my purse, things from the house and so on. In the end, he admitted that it was for heroin. He said he didn't know the drug was heroin when he first tried it – the girl who gave it to him called it something different, and it wasn't in a syringe. I think they smoked it or inhaled it or something.

Anyway, Adam promised he'd try and come off it, and we – his father and I – said we'd help as much as we could. We made an appointment with our doctor so that we could try to find a rehabilitation programme for him, and the three of us had an appointment on the Monday morning. But on the Saturday, Adam went out with some friends, and never came home again. As soon as the doorbell went, I knew he was dead. A policeman came to tell us. Adam had been found dead in a public toilet. What an awful place to die.'
(Sheila, whose son died of a heroin overdose, aged 18)

common in those who inject, and those who have other drugs, including alcohol, in their bloodstream. Most heroin users use a variety of other drugs.

When someone overdoses on heroin, they fall into what may appear to be a deep sleep, followed by coma. Friends often assume they will 'sleep it off' and will be okay in the morning, but if they do not receive medical attention quickly, the coma may be followed by death. In some cases, death from heroin use occurs because the person vomits while unconscious and inhales some of the vomit. This causes asphyxiation – suffocation due to blockage of the airways, so that oxygen cannot reach the lungs.

Additives

In addition to these risks, street heroin may be mixed with various substances, any one of which may be a poison itself. Many of the additives in street heroin, which can ass or brick dust, do not dissolve in ..lly they may clog the blood vessels that ...s, liver, kidneys or brain and the result of ......ection, death of small patches of cells as the bloou ...to the vital organs is seriously restricted, or even deaın of the user.

Effects of long-term use

Once someone starts using heroin regularly, they are highly likely to become addicted. The more heroin they use, the more the body adjusts to the dose, and as the body's tolerance increases, the person will need to take ever higher doses in order to achieve the same effect. Gradually, the 'high' or 'rush' diminishes and withdrawal symptoms, which can only be relieved by another 'fix' or 'hit' of the drug, kick in. Eventually, the user no longer experiences the euphoria that first made heroin attractive; they are now merely taking the drug in order to feel normal.

One of the major problems of heroin addiction is that it takes over the user's life. The person becomes so dependent on heroin that finding the next dose – and the means to pay for it – becomes their sole purpose in life. This can lead to a complete lack of interest in personal wellbeing, and may result in poor hygiene, inadequate diet and general ill-health. In addition, the user may take to crime in order to pay for the habit (more about this in Chapter 5).

Long-term heroin users are also more prone to depression and anxiety and, from an Australian study published in 2002, 14 times more likely than their peers to take their own lives. It is not clear whether this is the result of the drug itself or of other factors, such as the lifestyle of the user, or social or psychological problems that may have contributed to the person turning to drugs in the first place.

Other health risks
Breathing problems

Respiratory (breathing) problems are common in heroin users. These are conditions that affect the lungs, such as pneumonia, asthma and tuberculosis. Reasons for this may be the depressant effects of heroin on the respiratory system, the fact that blood vessels leading to the lungs are clogged with the additives in the heroin taken, and/or the poor health of the user.

Hepatitis

Hepatitis is a serious inflammation of the liver, caused by infection with any one of a number of hepatitis viruses. It can cause fever, fatigue, headaches and jaundice and can eventually trigger liver failure and cancer. Hepatitis infection is spread through contact with the bodily fluids of an infected person, so people who inject drugs and share needles are at particular risk. When someone injects, traces of their blood remain on the needle. If they have hepatitis, someone else using the same needle will inject infected blood straight into their own bloodstream. Hepatitis infection can also be passed by sexual intercourse.

Injecting

An injecting drug user (IDU) may tie something tight around their arm to make a vein become prominent so that they can inject the drug.

Hepatitis B and hepatitis C are common among injecting drug users (IDUs), and it is estimated that between 60 and 70 per cent of the world's IDUs are infected with the hepatitis C virus, while between 40 and 60 per cent are thought to be infected with hepatitis B.

Tetanus

Tetanus is an infection which enters the body through the puncture wound left by the needle. It acts on the nerves that control muscle activity, causing muscle stiffness, headache and fever. As the illness progresses, the muscles may go into painful spasms, and if the throat or chest is affected, breathing difficulties may occur and there is a risk of suffocation. Tetanus may kill if not treated quickly.

Collapsed veins

Repeated injecting can result in collapsed veins. Damage to some veins in an area means that blood is pumped there faster than the remaining veins can carry it away. So, for example, the arms, legs, hands or feet may become swollen and puffy, turn a blueish colour and be cold to the touch. Where veins are damaged there is insufficient blood flow to allow healing, and this damage is irreversible. The injection sites may become infected, causing boils or abscesses. Small scratches or knocks to the legs or feet are unable to heal properly and may become ulcerated. Ulcers are extremely painful open sores that can take months or even years to heal. If blood flow is severely restricted, areas of skin may even die, causing gangrene to set in. The affected parts may need to be amputated.

Another problem associated with collapsed veins is that the user soon runs out of veins in which to inject and resorts to injecting in other areas, including the groin, genitals or even the eyeball.

Abscesses

Abscesses are inflamed, pus-filled areas of flesh. They are usually swollen and painful and may feel hot to the touch. Abscesses develop as a result of unhygienic injecting: bacteria on the skin enter the body through the puncture made by the needle and set up an infection.

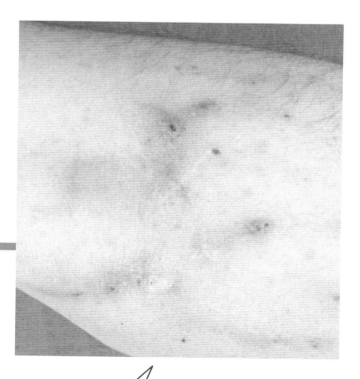

Irreversible damage
Scars left by injecting are likely to remain for life.

Skin problems

'Bad skin' is often associated with heroin use. It tends to be due more to the poor health and inadequate diet of the user than to the drug itself. Heroin users often appear pale and haggard-looking for the same reason.

HIV and AIDS

Like hepatitis viruses, the human immunodeficiency virus (HIV) is carried in bodily fluids and so can be transmitted through sharing needles with an infected person and through sexual intercourse. HIV can lead to acquired immune deficiency syndrome (AIDS). HIV infection gradually breaks down the body's immune system, making the infected person more susceptible to a number of infections and to certain types of cancer. When someone develops certain diseases and cancers as a result of HIV infection, they are diagnosed as having AIDS. Some conditions that occur as a result of HIV infection can be treated, but at present there is no cure and no vaccine.

'You want to know who does heroin around here? Just take a look. You can tell the scag-heads easy enough – they're the ones who look like corpses covered in scabs.' (Bernie, who stays in a hostel for young homeless men)

Fact file

According to the British Medical Association, half of all people infected with HIV will develop AIDS within 10 years, and will die from a related condition. The number of people who have become infected through needle-sharing varies worldwide. In the UK, around 3,000 people are thought to have become infected in this way. In the USA, in New York alone, there are an estimated 100,000 IDUs who are HIV-positive (this means that the HIV virus is present in their blood).

'When you're desperate, you just don't care'

Danny is 24 and has recently been told that he has full-blown AIDS. He is suffering from several illnesses, including cancer, and can no longer walk more than a few steps unaided.

'I don't know how long I've got,' says Danny, 'but put it this way: I'm not bothering to book a holiday next year.' He laughs, but the laughter turns to a painful coughing fit and a nurse puts an oxygen mask over his face. After a few minutes, he continues, his voice weak and rasping: 'I knew I was risking AIDS, but when you're desperate for a hit, you just don't care. You have to get the stuff into your veins somehow, and if that means sharing a needle, then that's what you do. You never think it'll happen to you, of course.

I started injecting because smoking didn't give such a kick any more. I'd heard that shooting up gave you a fantastic high, and it did – but only the first time. After that, it was never as good, and in the end, I was only doing it to stop myself feeling ill.

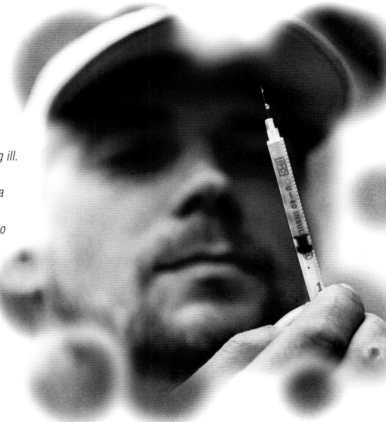

By the time I admitted I was a junkie, it was too late. I was diagnosed as HIV-positive two years ago. Since then, I've been ill most of the time, in and out of hospital. I'm not scared of dying, but I feel guilty for my mum and my sister. They get really upset when they visit, and my mum cries sometimes. I wish I hadn't been so stupid.'

Heroin and pregnancy

If a woman uses heroin while pregnant, she is more likely to have a miscarriage (where the fetus dies in the early stages of pregnancy and is expelled by the body). There is also an increased risk of the baby being born too early. This is known as premature delivery and makes the baby more vulnerable to infection and more likely to have breathing difficulties and development problems.

'I went into labour early, but they said my baby was already dead, because of the heroin. I had to go through the labour and delivery anyway. It was horrible. I know it was my fault she died.' (Gemma, aged 17)

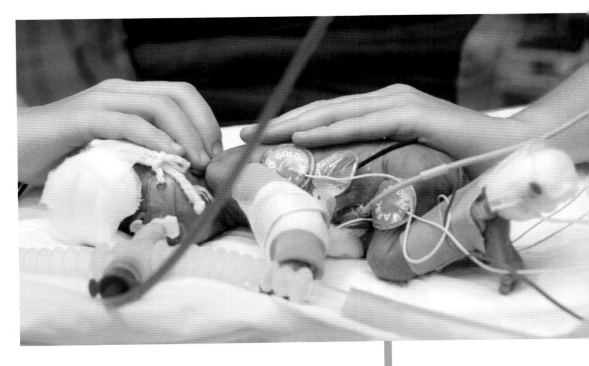

Babies born to heroin-addicted mothers are likely to be of low birth weight and tend to be in poor health generally, although this may be partly because of the mother's poor health and nutrition due to the lifestyle associated with heroin use, rather than to heroin itself. The babies are also more at risk of Sudden Infant Death Syndrome (SIDS), and if their mothers have used heroin intravenously, they may be born HIV-positive.

A dangerous start

A baby born prematurely needs intensive care. Its immune system is not fully developed and so infection is a great danger.

During pregnancy, heroin can cross from the mother's bloodstream, via the placenta (an organ in the womb), into the baby's bloodstream. This means that babies born to heroin-addicted mothers are born addicted, and therefore experience painful and distressing withdrawal symptoms in the first few days of life. Medical staff describe this as 'a terrible thing to see'.

'I saw a documentary on TV, where this woman was a heroin addict and she had a baby who was addicted too. I think it died.'
(Chloe, aged 15)

Expectant mothers who are addicted to heroin are often treated with methadone (see more about this in Chapter 6). Although this can still result in the baby having some dependency, it is generally less harmful than heroin. Pregnant women should not stop using heroin suddenly and without medical supervision, as sudden withdrawal can be fatal to the fetus.

The agony of a tiny baby

'I've been clean for over a year now. I'll never forget what it was like seeing Maisie in agony just after she was born. She just screamed and screamed, and whenever I went near her, she looked terrified. I didn't know what was wrong with her at first. Then a nurse told me that she was suffering from withdrawal. The nurse was horrible to me, calling me selfish and stupid, but I suppose I deserved it.

When I was pregnant, I was just wrapped up in myself, hanging out with the others in the squat where I lived and shooting up all the time. I had no contact with my family, and I never saw Maisie's dad again, so I didn't talk to anyone about my pregnancy. I didn't even see a doctor until I went into labour. I know it sounds crazy, but it really never occurred to me the damage I might be doing to my baby. They said I was lucky she made it – lots of babies don't. I love Maisie so much. I'm really trying to make it up to her now.'
(Hayley, aged 18)

5 The social consequences
A blight on family life

Once someone is in the grip of heroin addiction, it becomes increasingly difficult for them to continue with what we would regard as 'normal' life – studying or working, having relationships with family, friends and partners, taking care of their homes, looking after their health and appearance and enjoying interests or hobbies. Before long, heroin becomes the most important thing in their lives. This is because addiction means that, if they do not get their regular dose of the drug, they begin to suffer withdrawal symptoms which can be extremely painful and distressing. The result is that they spend most of their time and energy on finding the next dose and, of course, the money to pay for it.

It is estimated that the average heroin habit costs between £100 and £300 a week. Although occasional users may hold down a job, someone who becomes addicted will find it very difficult to work whilst coping with the physical effects of regular heroin use. Soon, therefore, the user finds they are spending considerably more on their heroin habit than they can earn or receive in benefits. They start to sell possessions – their CD player, their guitar, the camera their parents gave them for Christmas. Once all the large items have gone, they sell smaller items such as CDs, clothing – anything that will bring in a few pounds towards the next hit.

On the street
Many heroin users end up living on the street.

Once the user has sold all their own possessions, they often move on to stealing, at first from family and friends, perhaps taking money from their parents' homes or taking small items that they can sell. They may even convince themselves that they are only 'borrowing', and will replace what they have stolen later. They may move from this into burglary, robbery, fraud or prostitution. It is often the case that heroin users who have never previously broken the law turn to crime as a way to fund their habit.

The long-term social cost

Researchers at the University of California carried out a study lasting more than 30 years. They found that long-term heroin use resulted in higher levels of health problems, premature death, criminal behaviour and imprisonment, and reliance on state benefits.

Nearly 600 male heroin addicts were monitored from the early 1960s through to 1997. By that time, nearly half had died – a death rate of between 50 and 100 times higher than that among non-heroin users in the same age-range. The most common cause of death (21 per cent) was accidental overdose. Around 20 per cent of deaths were due to suicide, murder or accident. Most of the rest were due to liver disease, cancer and heart disease.

Heroin and the family

Heroin can be at the root of breakdowns in relationships between couples, parents and children, siblings and within the wider family. There is often a certain amount of deception and betrayal of trust involved in hiding and funding a heroin habit, and this causes problems within families. Parents may feel they can no longer leave their child alone in the house because he or she is likely to steal things. A wife or husband may feel they can never again trust a partner who has been lying to them.

'My brother's stuff was disappearing. He said he'd lent it to friends, but wouldn't say who. I knew he was selling it. Then he sold Mum's engagement ring – just after that, he admitted he was a heroin addict.' (Bethan, aged 16)

Also, the very nature of heroin addiction – a craving for the drug that becomes the focus of the person's life above all else – means that the heroin user has neither the time nor the energy to contribute to a normal relationship with family, friends or partner. For example, a recent posting on an internet heroin 'problem page' was from a young woman whose boyfriend of two years was an addict. She complained that, although he was trying to come off heroin, the drug seemed to be as important to him as she was. She said that heroin seemed almost like a 'mistress', a rival for his affection. One of the replies posted warned her that heroin dominates a person's life so much that it was highly likely that heroin was the boyfriend's greatest love, and that she, the concerned girlfriend, represented the cherished but less important 'mistress'.

For the children of heroin addicts, life is even more dismal. Apart from financial hardship, which can result in malnutrition and general poor health, there is a strong likelihood that the children will not be properly cared for. Heroin addicts, as we have seen, soon become focused mainly on finding and paying for heroin. Therefore, although they may love their children, they may be unable to care for them properly. Children

Looking away

Children whose parents are drug users may find strategies to cope with the distress it causes and the lifestyle it entails. Sadly they may become used to the fact that their parents are not 'there' for them.

may face hunger, lack of personal care, illness due to living in unhygienic surroundings and accidents through being left unattended, either because the parent is out finding heroin or is in a heroin-induced stupor ('on the nod'). There is also a risk of children accidentally taking heroin themselves or becoming infected with HIV or hepatitis if they come into contact with used syringes.

Children of addicts also suffer socially and educationally. Addicts often lose their homes, which may mean that they end up living in hostels or even on the streets. In some cases, their children may be fostered (looked after temporarily by another family) or taken permanently into the care of the local authority.

'It's hard deciding to take children away from their parents, but when you see kids going hungry, or having to call an ambulance because mummy's overdosed again, you have to consider putting them in care.' (Julie, social worker)

'She cries for her mummy'

Lynne's daughter, Molly, is 25 and has been addicted to heroin since she was 18. Molly's little girl, Jasmine, is six, and she now lives with Lynne.

'I thought things were getting better,' says Lynne. 'Molly was on a rehabilitation programme. She said she was determined to succeed, for Jasmine's sake. But I could see it wasn't working. She was in a daze half the time. When I went to visit, I couldn't believe the state of the place. She'd sold all the furniture to pay for heroin, and even the little silver mug I bought Jasmine for her christening. She was embarrassed when I found out, and I know she feels bad, but she can't stop herself.

One day, Jasmine saw me using a stock cube to make gravy. She said, 'I don't like stock soup. We have it all the time.' Molly had been feeding the child on stock cubes and hot water, and telling her it was soup! That's when I said Jasmine should come and live with me. It was heartbreaking to do that to my own daughter, to take her child away from her, but I couldn't watch my grandchild going hungry. I've begged Molly to get help, and she keeps promising that she will, soon. In the meantime, I hear Jasmine crying for her mummy, and I cry, too. For Jasmine, and for my daughter.'

The other major problem is the continuing cycle of drug abuse. It is estimated that up to 70 per cent of children with a parent who is addicted to drugs or alcohol will become addicted themselves. This may be because they have inherited a physical tendency to addiction, although there is little research on this, or it may be because they become so used to the lifestyle that goes with addiction that they naturally drift into similar patterns of behaviour to their parents.

Isolation

Someone whose parents are drug users is likely to try to keep it hidden. Doing so may make them seem unfriendly and they may become isolated.

'I wish my mum and dad would stop taking heroin. We've never got any money, and I'm too embarrassed to bring my friends home. When things are really bad, I have to live with my foster parents. They're nice, but I wish I could stay at my house.' (Rhys, aged 12)

Addiction can lead to misery and crime

Leah is 18 and has been working as a prostitute for over a year.

'I'm not proud of what I do. I didn't even realize what I was getting into. I've been hooked on smack for a couple of years now, and it was getting harder and harder to find the cash – I spend about £200 a week. Anyway, one day, I was really desperate. I was in a bad way, shivering and pains and stuff, and then this guy said if I slept with him, he'd sort me out. So I did. That happened a few times, and then he started introducing me to other guys who would pay me to do stuff, and I just sort of fell into it from there. It's a hell of a way to survive, but I don't know what else to do. I've been raped twice – they just think you're worthless and that you deserve it. I've also been arrested, and that's really scary. I'll get myself together one day, but I'm not sure how.'

Drug crimes and penalties

Buying, selling or using heroin is against the law. There are three main 'drug' crimes: possession, supply, and possession with intent to supply. How these crimes are defined remains unclear and the interpretation is up to the police and the courts, but even if someone gives a small amount of heroin to a friend and does not receive payment, this can still be seen as 'supply' and carries stiff penalties. In the UK, this means an unlimited fine and up to life imprisonment. For 'possession', which usually means an amount of at least one-sixteenth of an ounce, the maximum penalty is an unlimited fine and seven years imprisonment.

Crime can lead to misery and addiction

'I was fine before I went inside. I used to do a bit of dope now and again, or a few pills. But I would never have touched heroin. Then I got done for nicking. It was only a bit of stuff from work – video recorders, stereos, that sort of thing. But it was a second offence, so the judge sent me down. I got out after a year, but by that time, I was hooked. Heroin's the easiest drug to get in prison, and you have to do something to relieve the boredom. I don't know how it gets in, but there's no shortage.

Anyway, since I came out, my wife, Janine, has taken our little boy, Thomas – he's two – and moved back to her mum's. She says she doesn't want to see me any more, and she won't let me see Thomas, because she doesn't trust me not to shoot up while he's there. I swore I wouldn't, but if I'm totally honest, I probably would, if I needed it. We've lost our flat, and at the moment, I'm sleeping on friends' floors – my mum wouldn't have me back because of the drugs. And I'm losing mates fast – even my best mate from school said he doesn't want anything to do with me until I'm off the junk. Trouble is, what's the point of coming off it? I've got no job, no home, no wife and no kid, and my mum won't speak to me. What else is there?'
(Nick, aged 23)

In jail

Heroin users may end up in jail for possessing or supplying the drug, or for crimes committed in order to obtain it. However, some people say that it was in jail that they started using heroin.

Prison

Heroin has become the most widely used drug in prisons in the UK. It has been suggested that random drug testing within prisons may have contributed to the problem. If prisoners are found to have drugs in their system, they face punishments ranging from enforced segregation to having days added to their sentence, so obviously they are keen to avoid being caught. Heroin only stays in the body for around 78 hours, whereas cannabis, which many argue is less harmful and less addictive, can still be found in the body after four weeks. Drugs tests are therefore much less likely to pick up heroin than they are to find traces of cannabis, and this has made heroin the new 'drug of choice' in Britain's prisons.

Drug use is also a major problem in US prisons. Strict drug laws in the USA have resulted in a huge increase in the prison population, now almost two million. It is estimated that around 60 per cent of inmates are there for drug-related crimes. There are few studies in this area, so it is not possible to estimate the extent of heroin use specifically, but we do know that heroin addiction is a problem.

As needles are hard to come by in prison, injecting or tattooing (a popular pastime in prison) with used needles is common among inmates, and this has led to increased rates of HIV and hepatitis. There are calls for tighter security to prevent drugs getting into prisons, and more treatment programmes for inmates suffering from addiction.

Smuggling

Heroin is sometimes hidden in vehicles and brought into the country via ferries, or it may be concealed in luggage, clothing or, in some cases, the carrier's stomach, after being swallowed (see Chapter 2). In recent years there has been much publicity about people being talked into acting as 'mules' to smuggle fairly small amounts of heroin into a country. Young people in particular may be approached while on holiday and offered large amounts of money for what seems like 'easy' work. The idea is that ordinary holidaymakers are less likely to cause suspicion as they go through customs, so they simply conceal the drug in their suitcases, carry it through customs and then receive payment when they hand it over to the 'contact' who will meet them on their return. Due to recent world events, of course, airport security is tighter than ever, so the drug

smugglers may have to re-think their strategy. It may be that, as well as reducing the risk of a terrorist attack, increased security reduces the amount of illegal drugs being smuggled into the country.

The penalties for smuggling heroin are severe – up to life imprisonment or, in some countries, the death penalty. Apart from the risk of being caught, heroin carried inside the body is extremely dangerous, and people have died as a result of the packages bursting inside their stomachs.

Guns, gangs and gangster rap

There have always been links between drugs and violent crime, but the use of guns in drug-related crime is on the increase, with dealers battling it out on the streets over who is 'in charge' of certain areas – so called 'turf wars'. Drug-related gang crime, often involving teenagers as young as 14, is also on the increase, both in the UK and in the USA. These gangs are more common in low-income or deprived areas and are often made up of young people who have fallen outside of the 'normal' social system – for

Customs search

Customs officers may have specially trained dogs to help them find drugs concealed in people's luggage.

example, those who do not have a family home, whose home life is unhappy, who have serious problems at school, or do not attend school, and those who have a criminal record. For teenagers from an unstable, unhappy or abusive background, being a member of a gang can seem attractive – a sort of substitute family.

Research suggests that many gang members already have a criminal background, often involving theft, fraud, drug dealing and violent crime. The activities of gangs vary enormously, but drug dealing is common and often results in violence between rival gangs. Police believe that in some areas, youth gangs may be linked with adult criminal organizations who are involved in drug smuggling.

Drugs debate
People have differing views about whether rap lyrics about drugs promote heroin.

There has been much discussion recently about 'gangster rap', and whether the lyrics, which often dwell on violence and drug use, actually contribute to the rise in the use of heroin and other hard drugs. While it is true that some of these rap lyrics do seem to promote heroin, it is unlikely that they are directly responsible for the recent rise in use of the drug, particularly as pro-heroin lyrics have been around since the 1970s. However, some people argue that, if young people continually hear songs talking about and praising drug use as a 'cool' or even 'okay' thing to do, they may soon come to think of drug use as normal.

6 Prevention and treatment
A heroin-free future

Education and prevention

One of the best ways of reducing the devastation caused by heroin addiction is to prevent more people from trying the drug in the future. Hopefully this can be achieved by improved drugs education. Most people agree that drugs education is essential, but there is debate about what form it should take.

'Shock horror' tactics have sometimes been used in an attempt to frighten people away from using drugs. The parents of a 21-year-old British student, who died after injecting heroin, wanted pictures of their daughter's body to be used as 'a warning to others' about the dangers of heroin. Rachel Whitear's body was found on the floor of her flat three days after she died. Her flesh was bruised, swollen and discoloured, and she was still clutching the syringe she had used to inject herself with heroin. The harrowing picture has been included in an educational video – a move welcomed by the parents of other young people who have died from drug abuse.

However, research from around the world suggests that shock tactics don't work. Drugs education professionals feel that

Rachel's Story
The mother and step-father of Rachel Whitear hoped that a video about Rachel's death from heroin would discourage others from trying the drug.

the best way to teach children and teenagers about drugs is to give them plenty of information and to encourage open discussion.

Many organizations and pressure groups campaign for an improved approach. Some suggest that children should receive regular drugs education from the age of five. Experts agree that discussion about drugs should be part of all-round health education, at school and at home, and that it should also involve building up children's personalities and self-esteem. The idea is that, as you get older, this will help you to have the confidence to know what you think about the issues and the social skills to put your opinions across. Then, if you are faced with a situation where you are under pressure to behave in a way that might be dangerous, you will be able to say, 'Thanks, but this isn't for me.'

Saying 'No'
Having plenty of information about drugs and their effects will give you the confidence to say, 'No thanks, I don't want it.'

Lee, an ex-user, helps others

'Where I grew up, most kids were in trouble with the police by the time they were 13. There was no point in going to school – you knew you'd never get a job – so we just used to nick stuff, partly for the money, but mainly out of boredom.

We lived in a high-rise block on one of the roughest council estates in the country. All the kids on the estate did drugs. You'd start off sniffing aerosols, move on to cannabis and before long, heroin or crack. My mum's boyfriend, Mick, used heroin. He gave me some on my 16th birthday, for a "treat", and it felt really grown-up. My mum had a go at us, but we never took any notice.

By the time I was 18, I was an addict. Mick died of an overdose a few years later, and after that my mum begged me to get treatment. I tried a few times, but I kept dropping out. Then one day I was talking to a guy at the needle exchange and I thought, "He's right. This is stupid." So I got myself on a methadone programme and with lots of support, I came off heroin.

I've been clean for four years, and for the last two, I've been working for a drugs project. I'm training to be a qualified drug counsellor, and I think my experience helps – I know where they're coming from, what they're going through and so on. It's rewarding work and it's really turned my life around.'
(Lee, aged 25)

A social problem

Much research carried out both in the UK and the USA suggests that heroin use is more prevalent in deprived areas. Various studies show that heroin use was highest in the poorest households, for the age groups between 16 and 29; and that the use of any drug was higher among those who were unemployed. In a study of 11-15 year-olds, drug use was highest among those who felt they would not do as well in exams as they thought other people expected them to. Heroin use was more common in 16-19 year-olds who had achieved fewer qualifications.

People from areas where financial hardship is common are said to be 'socially excluded'. This means that they tend to

Environment
It seems that heroin use is more common in deprived environments.

have fewer opportunities for education, employment, health care and housing. Crime is more prevalent in these areas for obvious reasons. Living in conditions like these often leads to frustration, misery and depression, and it may be that this is when some people turn to drugs – as the research suggests, the use of heroin and other drugs is more common in these areas.

Many people believe that changes in society to improve education, employment prospects and housing would help to reduce social exclusion and therefore reduce heroin use. However, although there is clearly a link between heroin use and social exclusion, others argue that it's difficult to know which way round we should look at things: Does social exclusion cause people to turn to drugs? Or is it that drug use leads to social exclusion?

Fact file

It is extremely difficult to estimate the cost of heroin addiction, but one recent UK study showed the cost of policing drug misuse and providing treatment as around £3-4 billion. In the USA, the cost has been estimated at more than $20 billion. Research suggests that between 50 and 70 per cent of all recorded crime is in some way drug-related.

How can heroin addiction be treated?

As we have seen, addiction to heroin can wreck lives in terms of health, relationships, employment and housing. But addiction can be treated, and the sooner treatment begins, the more likely the user is to recover and stay off heroin. As heroin controls the user's life, becoming the only thing they are interested in, it can be difficult to get them to seek treatment, and so it may be some time before they get the help they need. Some people do seek treatment themselves, maybe because they realize their heroin use is out of control, or because of associated health problems.

Sometimes it is the family doctor who suggests treatment. Often, users are referred for treatment after ending up in a hospital accident and emergency department due to accidental overdose. In some cases, a hostel for the homeless or a local drug advice service puts users in touch with a treatment centre. Many others come through the criminal justice system, with treatment being a condition of their release or a part of their sentence. There are calls for more treatment programmes to be offered in prisons.

'This may sound stupid, but getting sent to jail was the best thing for me. Outside, I'd never have gone on a treatment programme, but inside, I got to think about my life and thought why not? Once I got started, I really wanted to succeed.' (Jay, aged 19)

Getting her life back – with Lee's help

'I only started going to the Project because someone told me they can help you get free heroin, but that turned out to be a load of rubbish. I've carried on going though, because they're really nice and they don't judge you. There's loads of information about different types of treatment and stuff, but they don't force you. I said I didn't want treatment at first, but I've been talking to Lee quite a lot, and he's just about convinced me.

I would like to come off it, but I suppose I'm a bit scared. I can't remember what it was like to get through the day without heroin, but Lee says you can get back to how you were before, and that you don't have to do anything you don't want to. I guess he knows what he's talking about, so I've agreed to be referred to a treatment centre. Lee's going to come with me for my first appointment. In a way, it's quite exciting – it means I might actually get my life back.' (Risana, aged 17)

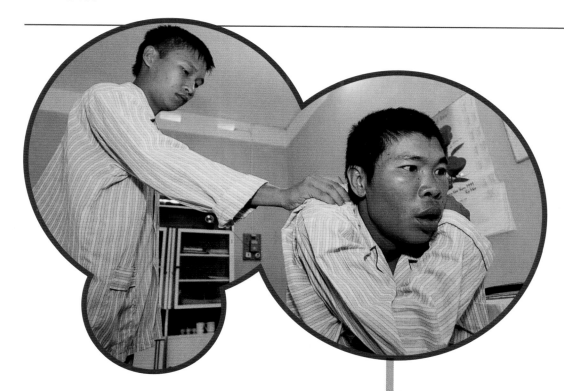

Withdrawal
These two men were photographed at a 'Re-education Centre' for heroin addicts in Hanoi, Vietnam. One is reassuring the other, as he suffers the symptoms of withdrawal from the drug.

Stopping heroin is very difficult for someone who has become dependent. Firstly, as the last dose of heroin leaves the body, the user starts to experience unpleasant and painful withdrawal symptoms. He or she knows that taking heroin will relieve those symptoms, and therefore longs for more heroin (this is called 'craving'). One method of treatment is to prescribe a controlled dose of another drug – a heroin substitute – that will relieve the withdrawal symptoms.

But even when the cravings and withdrawal symptoms are relieved, the user often finds it difficult to adjust to a heroin-free way of life. This usually involves mixing with different people and getting used to new daily routines, including new patterns of eating, sleeping and exercise. Because addicts have become dependent both on the drug itself and on a heroin user's lifestyle, experts believe that the most effective approach is a combination of medical treatment and counselling or behaviour therapy. Recovering from physical addiction and learning to live a heroin-free life is called 'rehabilitation', and a combination of treatments and therapy or counselling to help someone achieve this is often called a 'rehabilitation programme'.

Heroin addiction is described by professionals in the field as 'a chronic, relapsing condition'. This means that the person may have to make several attempts to come off heroin before they succeed. Roughly half of those who begin a treatment programme will drop out, and of those who complete the programme, around half will still be 'clean' (off heroin) two years later.

Methadone

The man-made opiate methadone is probably the most widely used treatment for heroin addiction. It works as a substitute for heroin by relieving withdrawal symptoms and suppressing cravings without producing the heroin 'high'. Some people argue that it merely creates another addiction, and it is true that patients can become dependent on it. However, the amount taken may be gradually decreased ('methadone reduction'). And even if the dosage remains the same ('methadone maintenance'), it is safer than heroin.

'It's great when someone says, "Thanks for your help, Martha. I'll never use heroin again." Some do, of course, but then we'll help them to get off it again.'
(Martha, a nurse at a rehabilitation clinic)

Like heroin, methadone is a dangerous drug with a high street value, so it is usually given at the clinic, in the form of a liquid medicine that only needs to be taken once a day. Correct dosage is vital – if the dose does not relieve the withdrawal symptoms, the patient is likely to go back to heroin to relieve their discomfort. This sets up the craving again and the user is back in the cycle of addiction.

Studies carried out in the USA show that between 65 and 85 per cent of people on methadone stay in treatment for a year or more, and the longer they do so, the better the outcome. Research shows that, in general, methadone patients are less likely to be involved in crime and more likely to be employed during treatment. There is also a considerable improvement in health and nutrition.

Heroin on prescription

Sometimes, when an addict has a high level of dependency, and other forms of treatment have not worked, doctors may decide to treat the person by prescribing heroin – this is the only way in which heroin may be used legally. Heroin prescribing is controversial, with some doctors suggesting that it merely keeps the person addicted. The advantage is that, although the person remains addicted, the amount of heroin they use, and its purity, can be controlled. They can also be given clean needles and syringes, reducing the risk of harm through injecting street heroin.

Someone on heroin prescriptions would be treated in a residential clinic or as a hospital inpatient, or they would have to visit the clinic each time they needed an injection – possibly three to four times a day. Only very rarely, once their condition had been stable for some time, would someone be allowed to use prescription heroin at home.

In the UK, only around one to two per cent of users in treatment receive heroin on prescription. Some senior police officers are in favour of more widespread prescribing, arguing that it may reduce crime. Health workers also point out that prescribing heroin keeps the user in touch with treatment services, so there may be a possibility of trying other forms of treatment again later.

Detoxification

This is where the patient undergoes medically supervised withdrawal, either as an inpatient or as an outpatient. Usually medication is used to relieve withdrawal symptoms, although it is possible to detox without medication. The idea is that once all traces of heroin have left the body, only the psychological addiction needs to be dealt with.

Counselling

There are some drug counsellors to whom people can go on a 'drop-in' basis, when they want help and advice. There is also a more formal, structured type of counselling where

Needle exchange schemes

Needle exchange schemes collect and dispose of used syringes and needles and offer new sterile syringes and needles in exchange. This reduces the risk of HIV, hepatitis and other blood-borne infections being spread among injecting drug users.

The schemes may also offer advice and counselling on drug problems and other health, social and welfare problems, as well as providing access or referral to other treatment services. Needle exchange schemes are also a good way of getting information to users about treatment and services available.

Some people argue that providing clean needles in this way increases intravenous drug use, though there is no evidence to support this. Research from several countries suggests that the schemes are effective and can significantly reduce risky behaviour.

treatment plans are made, goals are set and regular reviews are carried out. Counselling may be offered as part of a 'package', including medication, education and/or training, and management of other health problems. Studies show that those who have quality counselling are less likely to go back to heroin after treatment.

Structured or full-time outpatient programmes

These programmes offer an intensive form of rehabilitation, lasting around 12-16 weeks. They are often recommended in law courts as part of a 'sentencing order'.

Advice on the street
Needle exchange workers meet the heroin users in their own environment and may be able to encourage them to get treatment for their addiction.

If someone's crime appears to be linked to their heroin addiction, the judge may make their sentence conditional on their attending one of these programmes. Attendance is usually full-time, similar to college or working hours.

Programmes may focus on beating addiction, or on education or vocational training, or they may be targeted at particular types of heroin users, such as offenders. Many offer a combination of approaches. The aim is to provide access to information and advice and to help users develop other areas of their lives as they move back into society.

Where does treatment take place?

⊛ Users unable to manage their own treatment without constant support are treated as inpatients, supervised by medical staff, in a hospital or specialist clinic. Sometimes, a user undergoes detoxification in hospital and then has other forms of treatment as an outpatient.

⊛ Some users are treated at a residential centre other than a hospital or clinic. There may be medical supervision, but as part of a wider rehabilitation programme. A residential centre creates a 'false environment' in which users learn to do without heroin. When the user returns home, to their 'real environment', they may find it difficult not to return to old habits associated with heroin use.

⊛ Many people go for treatment as outpatients. To start with, they visit the clinic every day, to be given their medication. Later they may be able to move to using the medication at home. They may also go for counselling, sometimes over a period of several months.

How long does it take?

How long treatment takes depends on many factors, including how dependent the person is, what treatment is being used, where it is carried out, how much the person wants to come off heroin and whether they are a 'polydrug user' – someone who uses more than one drug at a time. Research suggests that the majority of heroin addicts are polydrug users. On average, an inpatient detoxification programme with medication to reduce withdrawal symptoms takes between two and seven weeks.

What works?

Different approaches suit different people, but in general, a combination of treatments is thought to be most effective for heroin addiction. Few studies have been completed on the effectiveness of the various forms of treatment, but those that are available tend to show a greater success rate among people undergoing inpatient or residential treatment.

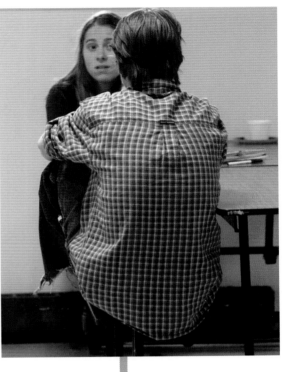

Counselling
Talking to a drug counsellor is a major part of recovering from addiction.

Heroin addiction is a cruel affliction that affects not only the individual, but their family and friends as well as society in general. Not only does it cause terrible illness, pain and death, but it takes away all sense of purpose and any sense of true happiness from those who become dependent. However, people can and do recover. Recovery can be difficult and traumatic, and the person may slip back several times before finally succeeding in becoming 'clean'. Those who have pulled themselves out of the cycle of addiction talk of being 'reborn' and of being given 'another chance at life'.

'When we saw Natasha in that hospital bed last year, her arms covered with track marks, her eyes sunken and hollow, we really didn't think she'd be with us today. We are so thankful that she got the help she needed, and that we have our daughter back.'

Let us hope that, with improved education and more open and free discussion about these issues, we will be able to help each other to find better ways to work through problems, and avoid sinking into the terrible cycle of addiction that has wrecked so many young lives.

Glossary

addiction	being dependent on a drug.
analgesic	a painkilling substance. There are many legal analgesics on the market, for example, paracetamol and aspirin.
asphyxiation	suffocation due to a blockage in the airways.
central nervous system	the brain and spinal cord, where 'messages' move from the brain to various parts of the body.
chronic	long-lasting or frequently recurring, such as in illness.
codeine	an analgesic drug derived from opium.
coma	deep unconsciousness caused by injury, illness or poison.
compulsive	needing to do something, being compelled, as in the sort of behaviour that occurs with addiction.
courier	someone who is paid to bring drugs into the country for someone else.
criminal justice system	the system whereby someone is arrested, prosecuted, sentenced and imprisoned.
dependence	powerful physical and/or psychological craving for a substance.
detoxification	the process of allowing the body to rid itself of toxins.
dopamine	brain chemical that regulates emotion.

endorphins	'feel-good' chemicals that occur naturally in the brain.
euphoria	intense feeling of pleasure, wellbeing or excitement.
fix	slang term for a dose of heroin.
gangrene	when body tissue dies due to bacterial infection or loss of blood supply.
hepatitis	inflammation of the liver.
hookah	pipe used to smoke opium.
immune system	the body's natural defence system, responsible for protection against and fighting of infection.
intravenous	into the vein (as in an injection).
junkie	slang term for a heroin addict.
labour	when a pregnant woman is 'in labour', it means that the process of childbirth has started. The labour describes the period from the first contraction (tightening) of the uterus until the baby is actually born.
laudanum	a mixture of opium, alcohol and spices, popular in the nineteenth century, and used recreationally by many people, particularly artists and writers.
malnutrition	the state of being undernourished as a result of a poor or inadequate diet.
morphine	an analgesic drug derived from opium.

narcotic	a drug which causes extreme drowsiness.
narcotism	the state of being sleepy or drowsy as a result of taking narcotic drugs.
opiates	a group of drugs that are derived from opium, including synthetic opiates, which have similar effects.
opioids	more general term for opiates.
opium	sticky substance that comes from the opium poppy.
pethidine	a synthetic analgesic opiate.
polydrug user	someone who uses more than one drug.
rehabilitation	the process of recovering, physically, psychologically and socially, from addiction.
relapse	the return of an illness or a condition such as addiction after apparent recovery.

rush	term used to describe the sudden feeling of euphoria experienced by a heroin user.
Sudden Infant Death Syndrome (SIDS)	the sudden unexpected death of a baby for no apparent reason.
synthetic	man-made, not a natural product.
syringe	glass or plastic cylinder with a needle attached for injecting heroin (or other substances) into the body.
tolerance	when the body adjusts to the presence of a substance, meaning that more is then needed to create a reaction.
withdrawal	the process of coming off an addictive substance.
works	equipment needed to inject heroin, e.g. teaspoon in which to heat the powder, syringe, needle, etc.

Resources

Organizations in the UK

National Drugs Helpline
Tel: 0800 776600
Confidential advice.

Drugscope
Tel: 020 7928 1211
Advice and information on all aspects of drug use.

ADFAM National
Tel: 020 7928 8900
Support and information helpline for families and
friends of drug users.

Release
Tel: 020 7729 5255
Confidential advice on drug use and related legal
issues.

Narcotics Anonymous UK
Helpline Tel: 020 7730 0009
Email: helpline@ukna.org
Self-help and support groups for recovering drug
users.

ChildLine
Telephone: 0800 1111
National 24-hour helpline for children and young
people in danger, distress or with any type of
problem.

National AIDS helpline
Telephone: 0800 012 322
Advice and information about HIV and AIDS-related
issues.

Further reading

Junk by Melvin Burgess (Puffin Teenage Books,
1996)
Novel about two teenagers who find themselves on
the dark and dangerous path of heroin abuse.
Described as 'gritty realism'.

Beauty Queen by Linda Glovach (Harper Collins,
1998)
Novel in diary form about a teenage girl's battle
with heroin addiction.

Need to Know: Heroin by Rob Alcraft (Heinemann,
2000)
Non-judgemental, non-patronizing information book
for teenagers.

*Different Like Me: A Book for Teenagers Who Worry
about Their Parent's Use of Alcohol/Drugs* by Evelyn
Leite and Pamela Espelan (Johnson Institute, 1989)
Offers practical advice and suggestions for teens
battling with a parent's addiction.

HAVERING
COLLEGE

LEARNING
RESOURCES
CENTRE

Index

CHAPTER 4

Dead in a public toilet

'Adam was a normal lad. He'd just left school and started work in a music store. It wasn't a wonderful job, but he seemed to like it. He made lots of friends, went to lots of parties – I was pleased that he was enjoying himself.

I had no idea he was into drugs until he started stealing from me, taking money out of my purse, things from the house and so on. In the end, he admitted that it was for heroin. He said he didn't know the drug was heroin when he first tried it – the girl who gave it to him called it something different, and it wasn't in a syringe. I think they smoked it or inhaled it or something.

Anyway, Adam promised he'd try and come off it, and we – his father and I – said we'd help as much as we could. We made an appointment with our doctor so that we could try to find a rehabilitation programme for him, and the three of us had an appointment on the Monday morning. But on the Saturday, Adam went out with some friends, and never came home again. As soon as the doorbell went, I knew he was dead. A policeman came to tell us. Adam had been found dead in a public toilet. What an awful place to die.'
(Sheila, whose son died of a heroin overdose, aged 18)

common in those who inject, and those who have other drugs, including alcohol, in their bloodstream. Most heroin users use a variety of other drugs.

When someone overdoses on heroin, they fall into what may appear to be a deep sleep, followed by coma. Friends often assume they will 'sleep it off' and will be okay in the morning, but if they do not receive medical attention quickly, the coma may be followed by death. In some cases, death from heroin use occurs because the person vomits while unconscious and inhales some of the vomit. This causes asphyxiation – suffocation due to blockage of the airways, so that oxygen cannot reach the lungs.

Additives

In addition to these risks, street heroin may be mixed with various substances, any one of which may be a poison itself. Many of the additives in street heroin, which can include powdered glass or brick dust, do not dissolve in the blood. Eventually they may clog the blood vessels that lead to the lungs, liver, kidneys or brain and the result of this can be infection, death of small patches of cells as the blood flow to the vital organs is seriously restricted, or even death of the user.

Effects of long-term use

Once someone starts using heroin regularly, they are highly likely to become addicted. The more heroin they use, the more the body adjusts to the dose, and as the body's tolerance increases, the person will need to take ever higher doses in order to achieve the same effect. Gradually, the 'high' or 'rush' diminishes and withdrawal symptoms, which can only be relieved by another 'fix' or 'hit' of the drug, kick in. Eventually, the user no longer experiences the euphoria that first made heroin attractive; they are now merely taking the drug in order to feel normal.

One of the major problems of heroin addiction is that it takes over the user's life. The person becomes so dependent on heroin that finding the next dose – and the means to pay for it – becomes their sole purpose in life. This can lead to a complete lack of interest in personal wellbeing, and may result in poor hygiene, inadequate diet and general ill-health. In addition, the user may take to crime in order to pay for the habit (more about this in Chapter 5).

Long-term heroin users are also more prone to depression and anxiety and, from an Australian study published in 2002, 14 times more likely than their peers to take their own lives. It is not clear whether this is the result of the drug itself or of other factors, such as the lifestyle of the user, or social or psychological problems that may have contributed to the person turning to drugs in the first place.

Other health risks
Breathing problems
Respiratory (breathing) problems are common in heroin users. These are conditions that affect the lungs, such as